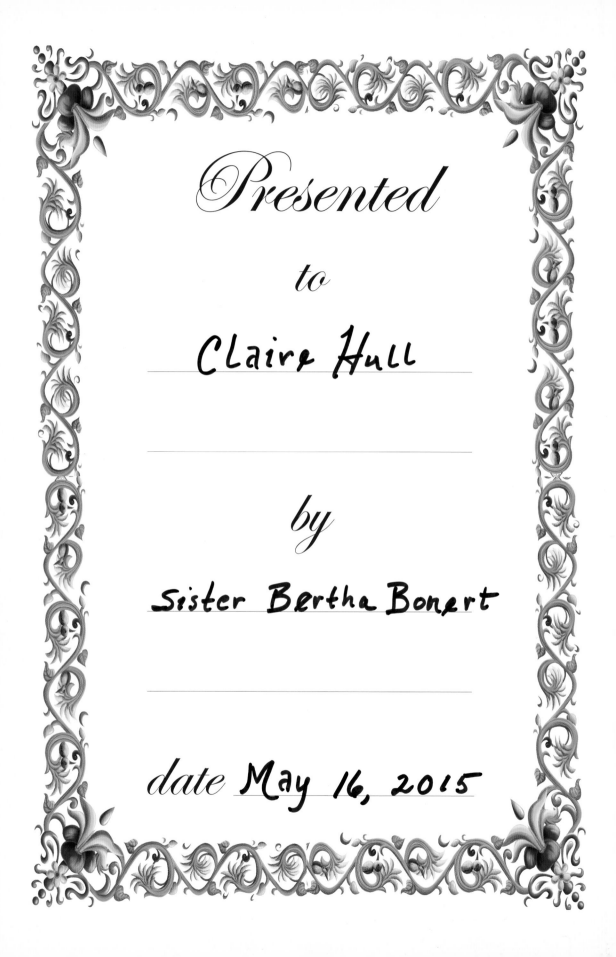

Presented

to

Claire Hull

by

Sister Bertha Bonert

date May 16, 2015

ST. JOSEPH ILLUSTRATED

BOOK OF SAINTS

CLASSIC LIVES OF THE SAINTS FOR CHILDREN

•

By Rev. Thomas J. Donaghy

•

ILLUSTRATED IN FULL COLOR

CATHOLIC BOOK PUBLISHING CORP.
New Jersey

Nihil Obstat: Rev. Msgr. James M. Cafone, M.A., S.T.D., *Censor Librorum*
Imprimatur: ✠ Most Rev. John J. Myers, J.C.D., D.D., *Archbishop of Newark*

The Nihil Obstat and Imprimatur are official declarations that a book or pamphlet is free of doctrinal or moral error. No implication is contained therein that those who have granted the Nihil Obstat and Imprimatur agree with the contents, opinions or statements expressed.

(T-765)

ISBN 978-1-941243-07-7

Contents

Contents

Foreword

In a small country church where I first attended Mass and received First Reconciliation and Holy Communion, I was fascinated by two rather large statues of our Blessed Mother and St. Joseph. One could easily understand that these were images of holy people. As we grew older, we came to realize that Our Lady, St. Joseph, and thousands of others live with God in heaven.

In school, we learned more and more about the Saints, and we began to realize that their pictures and statues gave us a good idea of where and when they lived. In hearing and reading their stories, we came to know and understand that even though the Saints grew up in different countries and cultures, the way they lived and loved God and neighbor was something we could do.

Today, we have many role models in a variety of different fields and professions, as well as, of course, our parents and siblings. Adults often ask children the age-old question, "What do you want to be when you grow up?" It is a reasonable question. Sometimes it starts us thinking about our personal futures. The beauty is that no matter what we want to be, we can carry out our plans and dreams and still strive to be Saints.

It is important to read and recall the good lives of Saints, and to pray to one or several of these holy people each day. This book can easily help us follow the Saint or Saints we really want to imitate.
                                        —*Father Thomas J. Donaghy*

Our Lady, Queen of Heaven and Earth

On October 11, 1954, His Holiness, Pope Pius XII, in his encyclical letter, *Ad Caeli Reginam*, decreed and instituted the feast of the Queenship of the Blessed Virgin Mary to be celebrated throughout the world every year. He declared that the Church has believed in Mary's Queenship from the earliest centuries and that this belief rests on Holy Scripture and tradition.

Mary is Queen of all "since she brought forth a Son, Who at the very moment that He was conceived, was . . . King and Lord of all things." Further, "as Christ is our Lord and King by a special title because He redeemed us, so the Blessed Virgin [is our Lady and Queen] because of the unique way in which she has cooperated toward our redemption by giving of her own substance, by offering Him willingly for us, and by desiring, praying for, and bringing about our salvation in a singular manner."

The significance of Mary's Queenship for contemporary times is that her participation in the work of her Son rouses hope and expresses a merciful and ongoing love. In looking to Mary, the faithful can find in her the secret to their own royal identity as children of God and the model for giving the Lord a greater place in their lives.

August 22

St. Elizabeth Ann Seton

Elizabeth Seton was born on August 28, 1774, to a wealthy and distinguished New York Episcopalian family. She lost her mother at an early age, leaving her upbringing and education to her father. She was a voracious reader who enjoyed the Bible. In her youth and young adulthood, she was a faithful, fervent adherent of the Episcopal Church.

At nineteen, she married William Magee Seton. Their happy union produced five children, yet their life together was plagued by suffering and illness. Elizabeth and her sick husband traveled to Leghorn, Italy, in the hope that the location would improve his condition, but William died there.

After the loss of her husband, Elizabeth was comforted by life-long friends, the Filicchis, who acquainted her with Catholicism. In 1805, she joined the Catholic Church.

She established her first Catholic school in Baltimore in 1808, thus beginning the parochial school system in America. In 1809, she established a religious community in Emmitsburg, Maryland, soon becoming known as Mother Seton. Her small community of teaching sisters grew and expanded throughout the country, eventually becoming the Sisters of Charity.

Elizabeth died on January 4, 1821. She was beatified in 1963, and then canonized on September 14, 1975, by Pope Paul VI, making her the first American-born Saint.

January 4

St. Agnes

At thirteen, St. Agnes died around 304 and became one of the best known and most highly regarded of the Roman martyrs.

The *Acts* of her passion are not considered entirely reliable, but they provide some details. Young Roman noblemen vied with one another to obtain her hand in marriage. She refused them all, saying that she had chosen a Spouse Who could not be seen with mortal eyes. Her suitors, hoping to shake her constancy, accused her of being a Christian.

Brought before a judge, Agnes remained unswayed. Fires were kindled, instruments of torture were placed before her eyes, but she viewed them with fearless calm. Sent to a house of prostitution, she inspired such awe that not one of the wicked youths of the city dared approach her.

Agnes came forth from this den of infamy a pure spouse of Christ. Her most prominent suitor was so enraged that he further incited the judge against her. The heroic virgin was condemned to be beheaded. "She went to the place of execution," says St. Ambrose, "more cheerfully than others go to their wedding."

Amid the tears of the spectators, she went to meet the Immortal Spouse Whom she had loved better than her life. Agnes was buried on the Via Nomentana, and Constantine erected a church in her honor.

January 21

St. Francis de Sales

St. Francis, son of the Count de Sales, was born in 1567. Early on, he desired to be a priest. Around age eleven, he was sent to Paris to study philosophy and theology. He went on to the University of Padua, where he received a doctorate in both canon and civil law.

Afterward, his parents reluctantly consented to have Francis enter the priesthood. He later took upon himself the mission of Chablais, where Calvinism had deep roots. Francis worked tirelessly and won many converts. While engaged in these efforts, he was appointed coadjutor to the Bishop of Geneva, whom he succeeded in 1602.

He labored zealously in his diocese and elsewhere for the clergy and the people. Francis also composed several instructive and uplifting works for the faithful. In 1610, he founded the Order of the Visitation, with the help of St. Jane Frances de Chantal.

Amid his constant pastoral work Francis found time to write the book that has made him known to succeeding ages: *Introduction to a Devout Life*. It shows how ordinary life can be sanctified; no problem was too small for its author to address. His one concern was how to lead the reader to the love of God and the imitation of Christ.

His death in 1622 was followed by canonization in 1665.

January 24

St. Thomas Aquinas

St. Thomas, born in 1226, was the son of the Count of Aquino. At the age of five, he was placed under the care of the Benedictines of Monte Cassino. There Thomas surpassed all his fellow pupils in learning and in virtue.

When he was older, he renounced the things of this world and resolved to enter the Order of St. Dominic—despite family opposition. At seventeen, Thomas joined the Dominicans of Naples. God rewarded his faithfulness by conferring upon him the gift of perfect chastity, earning him the title "Angelic Doctor."

He studied in Cologne under St. Albert the Great. Here he was nicknamed the "Dumb Ox" because of his silent ways and huge size, but he was, in fact, a brilliant student. At twenty-two, he was appointed to teach in Cologne and there began to publish his first works. Thomas had become a priest before receiving his doctorate at age thirty-one.

In 1261, Urban IV called him to Rome to teach, but he positively declined to accept any high Church position. Thomas was both a prolific writer and an effective preacher. Clement IV offered to make him the Archbishop of Naples, but he refused the honor.

He left the great monument of his learning, the *Summa Theologica*, unfinished at his death in 1274. He was canonized in 1323 by Pope John XXII.

January 28

St. John Bosco

St. John Bosco was born on a poor farm near Turin, Italy, in 1815. At a very young age, he was out on the hillside tending sheep. When he was about nine, he expressed the desire to become a priest. He then finally began his formal education, going to school for six months and spending six months in the fields.

The day before he entered the seminary, as he stood robed in his clerical dress, his mother said: "To see you dressed in this manner fills my heart with joy. But remember that it is not the dress that gives honor to the state, but the practice of virtue. If at any time you come to doubt your vocation, I beseech you, lay it aside at once. I would rather have a poor peasant for my son than a negligent priest."

This "Apostle of Youth" founded the Salesian Society of St. Francis de Sales and the Daughters of Mary Help of Christians. His life's work was consecrated to the care of young boys and girls.

John Bosco's success with youth flowed from showing them much care, imposing few restraints, manifesting true concern for their development, and giving them personal and religious encouragement.

He died in 1888 and was canonized in 1934 by Pope Pius XI.

January 31

St. Margaret of Cortona

In 1247, Margaret of Cortona was born in Laviano in Tuscany, where her father was a farmer. Motherless at seven, she and her stepmother were always at odds. Margaret left home at a young age to live with a youth from a nearby town. Though unmarried, she bore him a son. After a few years, the young man was murdered.

A regretful Margaret returned home with her son, but they were unwelcome. They then sought help from the Friars Minor at Cortona. In time, she asked for forgiveness for her past life.

Margaret earned a living by caring for sick women. Later, she worked without pay, serving the sick poor, living on alms alone. Eventually, she joined the Third Order of St. Francis. Subsequently, her son also joined the Franciscans. Margaret had a deep prayer life and was said to communicate directly with Jesus.

In 1286, she was granted a charter to work for the sick poor permanently. Others joined Margaret, and they later were given special status as a Congregation called the Poverelle ("Poor Ones").

For years, Margaret preached against vice. She also showed extraordinary love for the Eucharist and Christ's Passion. Divinely warned of the day and hour of her death, she died on February 22, 1297. She was canonized in 1728 by Pope Benedict XIII.

February 22

St. Dominic Savio

St. Dominic Savio was born in Riva, Italy, in 1842. His faith was important to him at an early age. By the time he was five, Dominic had already learned to serve Mass. When he was twelve, he visited St. John Bosco at the Oratory school that St. John had founded and told him of his desire to become a priest. Among the young boys St. John had helped form, Dominic held a special place in the Saint's heart. It actually was St. John Bosco who wrote the story of Dominic's life.

Dominic's holiness was readily apparent. His schoolmates found him to be kind, generous of spirit, and cheerful. He worked hard to be a good student. Dominic also loved to pray and did so fervently. Unfortunately, due to poor health, he could no longer remain at the Oratory school and had to return home after being there for only two years.

His joyful spirit remained intact, however, and he continued to keep the rules he had written on his First Communion Day: (1) I will go to Confession and Communion often; (2) I will keep holy the Feast days; (3) Jesus and Mary will be my best friends; (4) I will rather die than commit a sin.

Dominic was only fifteen when he died. This model for youth became a Saint in 1954.

March 9

St. Patrick

The date and place of St. Patrick's birth are uncertain. He was born about 389. When he was sixteen, he was carried to Ireland as a captive. Despite the harshness of the life there, he not only held on to his Faith but also learned the science of prayer and contemplation.

After six years, he miraculously escaped and returned home. In a dream, Patrick was told to go back and Christianize Ireland. He prepared to do so by studying in the monastery of Lerins from about 412 to 415 and was ordained about 417.

In 431, after a time of hesitancy by his superiors in entrusting such a mission to him, they sent him to assist Bishop Paladius in Ireland. When the Bishop died, Patrick was consecrated Bishop in 432, after receiving the approval of Pope Celestine I. He planted the Faith everywhere in Ireland, despite the hostility of the Druids, even converting several members of the royal family.

In winning a pagan nation for Christ, Patrick established many monasteries for men and women and made Ireland famous for its seats of piety and learning. In the ensuing centuries, Irish monks carried the Faith to England, France, and Switzerland.

Patrick died on March 17, 461, leaving behind his *Confessions*, which give a vivid picture of a great man of God.

March 17

St. Joseph

St. Joseph, the pure spouse of the Blessed Virgin Mary and foster-father of Jesus, was descended from the royal house of David. He is the "just man" of the New Testament, the lowly village carpenter of Nazareth, who among all men was the one chosen by God to be the husband and protector of the Virgin Mother of Jesus Christ, God Incarnate. To his faithful, loving care was entrusted the childhood and youth of the Redeemer of the world.

Joseph was gifted with abundant virtues. In purity of heart, in chastity of life, in humility, patience, fortitude, gentleness, and manliness of character, he reveals to us the perfect model of the true Christian.

Poor and obscure in this world's possessions and honors, he was rich in grace and merit. Because Joseph was the divinely appointed head of the Holy Family, which was the beginning of the great Family of God—the Church—Pope Pius IX solemnly proclaimed him Patron of the Universal Church on December 8, 1870. Thus, from his throne of glory in heaven, St. Joseph watches over and protects the Church.

From that time, his Feast on March 19 has been celebrated as one of high rank. Besides the Feast of March 19, there is the Feast of St. Joseph the Worker on May 1, promulgated in 1955.

March 19

St. Bernadette of Lourdes

St. Marie Bernadette Soubirous was born to a poor family at Lourdes, France, in 1844. At fourteen, she witnessed eighteen apparitions of Our Blessed Lady there. In the first, as Bernadette was gathering firewood, a beautiful Lady, dressed in blue and white, stood before her in a cave, or grotto. She smiled at Bernadette and asked her to say the Rosary with her.

Our Lady asked Bernadette to spread important messages to the world. People were to do penance for their sins and pray. The Mother of God revealed the miraculous healing powers of the waters at Lourdes. When she asked Bernadette to scrape the earth there, a spring started to flow. The Blessed Virgin also told Bernadette that she is the Immaculate Conception.

In 1866, Bernadette joined the Sisters of Charity at Nevers, taking her perpetual vows in 1878. Her contemporaries admired her humility and the authentic character of her testimony about the appearance of the Blessed Virgin.

Nevertheless, she had to endure many severe trials during her religious life and exhibited heroic patience in sickness. She died in 1879 at the age of thirty-five and was canonized in 1933 by Pope Pius XI.

April 16

St. Catherine of Siena

St. Catherine, born in 1347, consecrated her virginity to God in her childhood. However, her parents wished to see her married and challenged her will. She bore her trials with fortitude and joy, continuing her resolve to give herself entirely to God. When her parents relented, she was left free to follow her pious inclinations.

At eighteen, she received the habit of the Third Order of St. Dominic. During the great pestilence, she cared for the infected. Meanwhile, her exhortations converted thousands.

In 1376, she went to Avignon to seek peace between Pope Gregory XI and the Florentines, whom he had strongly sanctioned for joining in a conspiracy against the temporal possessions of the Holy See in Italy. She also aided his return to Rome and exhorted him to contribute whole-heartedly toward peace in Italy.

Witnessing the beginning of the Great Schism, she wrote to the cardinals who caused it and to several princes, seeking to avert the terrible evil.

At thirty-three, Catherine died on April 29, 1380. She was canonized in 1461 by Pope Pius II.

Long regarded as one of the finest theological minds in the Church—as is shown by her outstanding work, *Dialogue*—she was declared a Doctor of the Church by Pope Paul VI in 1970.

April 29

St. Isidore the Farmer

St. Isidore was born in Madrid, Spain, in the latter part of the eleventh century, probably in the year 1070. His poor but faithful parents named him after the famed St. Isidore of Seville, Bishop and Doctor of the Church.

For the greater part of his life, he was employed as a laborer on a farm owned by a wealthy nobleman of Madrid, which was located outside the city. Without fail, he attended daily Mass. Since this practice sometimes led Isidore to arrive late at his work, neighbors of his employer accused him of neglecting his duty. A mild-mannered man, Isidore defended his actions simply by acknowledging his service and obedience to his God and Master.

The simplicity of his life was marked by his prayer and his work. Not only was he blessed by heavenly visions, but it is said that his faithful commitment to attending Mass was rewarded by the presence of angels who assisted him in plowing the fields he tended.

He was married to a peasant girl named Maria Torribia who shared his values of faith, hard work, and commitment to those who were even less fortunate than they were.

Isidore died in 1130 and was declared a Saint in 1622 by Pope Gregory XV. The Church honors him as the patron of farmers.

May 15

St. Rita of Cascia

St. Rita, born at Spoleto, Italy, in 1381, begged her parents at an early age to allow her to enter a convent. They instead arranged a marriage for her.

Rita's husband had a violent temper and taught their two sons his harsh ways. Nonetheless, Rita tried to perform the duties of wife and mother faithfully and to pray and receive the Sacraments frequently.

After nearly twenty years of marriage, her husband was murdered. Before he died, however, Rita's prayers led him to repent.

She forgave her husband's killers, but she feared that her sons might exact revenge for his death. Rita prayed to God that they not resort to murder. Due to illness, both of her sons died shortly after their father.

Now alone, Rita thought of fulfilling the longings of her youth by seeking admission to the religious life. After overcoming formidable difficulties, she was admitted to the convent of the Augustinian nuns in Cascia and began a life of obedience and charity.

Rita's great devotion to Christ Crucified led her to ask to suffer like Him. While in prayer before a crucifix, a thorn from His crown of thorns struck her on the forehead, leaving a deep wound that did not heal.

Rita died on May 22, 1457, and was canonized in 1900.

May 22

St. Dymphna

St. Dymphna was born in Ireland in the seventh century. Her father, Damon, was a pagan chieftain of great wealth and power. Her mother was a woman of uncommon beauty and a devout Christian.

When she was just fourteen, Dymphna lost her mother. Damon is said to have become literally mad with grief at the death of his wife. Perhaps as a means to cope with his despair, he decided to send messengers throughout his own and other lands to find a woman both of noble birth and resembling his wife, who would consent to marry him. When no one suitable could be found, his unscrupulous advisers told him to marry his own daughter.

Upon hearing this proposal, Dymphna fled from her castle together with St. Gerebran, her confessor, and two other friends. Damon sought them out and discovered them in Belgium. He gave orders that the priest's head be cut off. Then Damon tried to persuade his daughter to return to Ireland with him as his wife. When she refused, being committed to her vow of purity, he drew his sword and struck off her head. She was then only fifteen years of age.

A virgin and martyr, Dymphna is the patroness of the mentally ill. Many miracles have taken place at her shrine in Gheel, Belgium.

May 30

St. Joan of Arc

On January 6, 1412, Joan of Arc was born to pious parents of the French peasant class. At a very early age, she heard voices: those of St. Michael, St. Catherine, and St. Margaret. At first, the messages were personal and general. In May 1428, however, her voices told Joan to go to the king of France and help him to reconquer his kingdom.

King Charles gave the seventeen-year-old girl a small army, with which she raised the siege of Orléans on May 8, 1429. She then enjoyed a series of spectacular military successes, during which the king was able to enter Rheims and return to his throne.

In May 1430, Joan fell into the hands of the British. After nine months of imprisonment, she was tried at Rouen, where she unwittingly was trapped into making a few damaging statements. When she refused to retract the assertion that it was the Saints of God who had commanded her to do what she had done, she was condemned to death as a heretic and burned at the stake on May 30, 1431. She was a mere nineteen years old.

Some thirty years later, Joan was exonerated of all guilt, and she ultimately was canonized in 1920 by Pope Benedict XV, making official what people had known for centuries.

May 30

St. Anthony of Padua

St. Anthony was a native of Lisbon, Portugal, where he was born in 1195. At an early age, his parents arranged his education at the Cathedral of Lisbon. At fifteen, he joined the Order of Regular Canons of St. Augustine, and, after two years, he was sent to the monastery of that Order at Coimbra.

He had lived in this house eight years, intent on his studies, when the relics of five Franciscan martyrs were brought to Coimbra. This event was a turning point for Anthony who was inspired to become a Franciscan. In 1221, he was accepted into the Franciscan Order.

After some time, he set out for Africa to preach to the Moors, but illness obliged him to return home. On the way, his ship was driven to Sicily in a storm. From there, he went to see St. Francis in Assisi, where a general chapter meeting of the Order was in progress. The Franciscans soon learned his value as a professor of theology and as a preacher.

In time, he gave up teaching to devote himself solely to preaching, for he was an accomplished orator. In this work, he traveled through France, Spain, and Italy. Anthony spent his later life in Padua and died on June 13, 1231. Pope Gregory IX canonized him the following year. *June 13*

St. Thomas More

St. Thomas More was born at London in 1478. Classically educated in his youth, he later entered Oxford to study law. A legal career that took him to Parliament followed. In 1505, Thomas married his beloved Jane Colt. She died young, and he married a widow, Alice Middleton, for the sake of his four children.

His house in Chelsea became a center of intellectual life. Thomas himself became a leading light of his time, honored for his intellect and scholarship. He composed poetry, history, treatises, devotional literature, and Latin translations. By 1516, he wrote his world-famous book *Utopia*.

Henry VIII appointed him to a succession of high posts, finally naming him Lord Chancellor in 1529. He resigned in 1532, when Henry persisted in holding his own opinions regarding marriage and the supremacy of the Pope.

Thomas spent the rest of his life writing, mostly in defense of the Church. In 1534, with his close friend, St. John Fisher, he refused to render allegiance to the king as the Head of the Church of England and was confined to the Tower. More than a year after John Fisher's execution, he was convicted of treason.

He told the court that he could not go against his conscience. Thomas was beheaded on July 6, 1535, and canonized in 1935 by Pope Pius XI.

June 22

St. John the Baptist

The Feast of the Nativity, or birthday, of St. John the Baptist, the precursor of the Messiah who was born six months before Him, is observed on June 24, and it is one of the oldest Feasts in the liturgy of the Church. He was the son of Zechariah and Elizabeth, a cousin of the Blessed Virgin Mary. What we know of this Saint and great prophet, from his sanctification before his birth to his martyrdom under King Herod, is set down in Holy Scripture.

Thirty years after the birth of Jesus, John began his mission on the banks of the Jordan. He was the last of the prophets of the Old Covenant. His work was to prepare the way and announce the coming of the long-expected Messiah, the Redeemer. He had the honor of baptizing Jesus.

Shortly afterward, John rebuked Herod Antipas, the ruler in Galilee and Perea, for taking as his wife Herodias, the wife of the ruler's brother, Philip. In retaliation, John was cast into prison. He was then beheaded by order of Herod at the instigation of Herodias.

June 24

St. Peter the Apostle

St. Peter was a Galilean fisherman named Simon. His brother, Andrew, introduced him to Christ. They likely learned of Him from John the Baptist. Simon became His disciple, ultimately giving up everything to follow Him. Christ changed his name to Peter (meaning Rock) and made him the Rock on which he would build His Church. After His Resurrection, Jesus made Peter the head of the Apostles and the first Pope.

The Gospels speak about Peter more than any other Apostle. He often was honored and frequently acted as spokesman for the other Apostles. Mention also is made of his shortcomings.

After the Ascension, Peter began his work as head of the Church. He directed the election of Matthias, delivered the first public Apostolic sermon, cured a man lame from birth, and received a Divine commission to receive Gentiles into the Church. He presided at the Apostolic Council of Jerusalem in the year 49, when it was officially declared that Gentile converts to the Faith were not subject to the Jewish law of circumcision. Afterward, he went to Antioch, where it was decided that Christians were not bound to observe the Mosaic dietary laws.

In the last year of Nero's reign, 67, Peter was crucified with his head downward, at his own request, not deeming himself worthy to die as did Christ. *June 29*

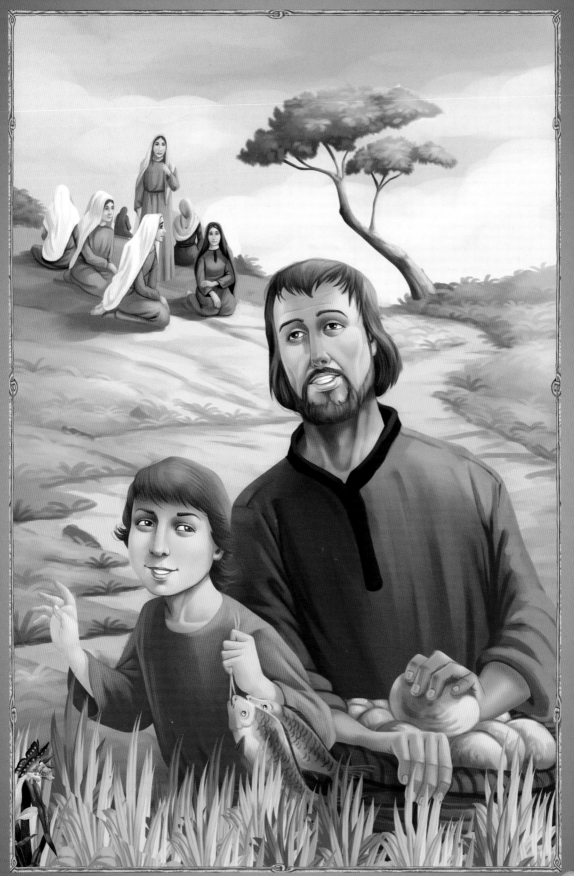

St. Paul the Apostle

St. Paul, a devout Jew from Tarsus, was on his way to Damascus to arrest Christians when, having fallen to the ground and surrounded by light, he heard Jesus ask why he was persecuting Him. After his dramatic conversion and Baptism, he became a zealous Apostle of Christ.

Once he had prepared in Arabia for his future missionary activity, he journeyed to Damascus, Jerusalem to meet Peter, and Antioch. Following these travels, he crisscrossed the cities of Asia Minor in which he established among the Gentiles

communities of Christians. Because of distrust of him and of his message that Jesus is the Son of God, he met with resistance from his enemies, faced imprisonment, and endured beatings. Even the elements plagued him as he encountered shipwreck during his travels.

Despite these trials, Paul was embraced by those he converted among the Corinthians, Ephesians, Galatians, and Romans. To help them sustain their new Faith, he wrote letters of encouragement, direction, and admonishment. These letters continue to teach the faithful even to this day.

After a second imprisonment in Rome, Paul was beheaded in 67.

June 29

Bl. Junípero Serra

Miguel José Serra was born on the island of Majorca on November 24, 1713, and took the name of Junípero when in 1730 he entered the Franciscan Order. Ordained in 1737, he taught philosophy and theology at the University of Padua until 1749.

At the age of thirty-six, Junípero landed in Mexico City on January 1, 1750, and spent the rest of his life working for the conversion of the peoples of the New World.

In 1768, Father Serra took over the missions of the Jesuits (who had been wrongly expelled by the government) in the Mexican province of Lower California and Upper California (modern California). A tireless worker, this holy man was responsible in large part for the foundation and spread of the Church on the West Coast of the United States, when it was still mission territory.

Father Serra founded twenty-one missions and converted thousands of Indians. The converts were taught sound methods of agriculture, cattle-raising, and arts and crafts.

A dedicated religious and missionary, Junípero had a penitential spirit and practiced austerity in many of his everyday activities. Father Serra died on August 28, 1784, after years of tireless labor. He was beatified by Pope St. John Paul II on September 25, 1988. His statue, representing the State of California, is in National Statuary Hall.

July 1

St. Benedict

The Patriarch of Western monasticism was born in Italy about 480. Gregory's *Dialogues* provide most of what is known of St. Benedict's life. In his youth, he saw the corrupt world around him, which led him to leave home to live a hermit's life of penance and prayer outside Rome in a cave in the mountain of Subiaco.

His reputation for sanctity drew disciples to him. He erected monasteries in which they lived life in community—praying, clearing the land, planting crops, teaching school, feeding the poor—under a prescribed Rule. In 529, he left Subiaco for Monte Cassino, near Naples, and there founded the great Abbey that became the center of religious life in Europe.

St. Scholastica, his sister, was the first Benedictine nun. She presided over a monastery of nuns near Monte Cassino.

The principles of the Benedictine Rule became the spiritual foundation for all subsequent Western religious orders and congregations. His Rule shows the way to religious perfection by practicing self-conquest, mortification, humility, obedience, prayer, silence, prudence, moderation, stability, retirement, and detachment from the world. His monastic way of life was orderly, workable, and complete.

Benedict died March 21, 547, standing before the altar of Monte Cassino. It is said that his monks held up his arms in prayer as he received the Eucharist before he died. *July 11*

St. Kateri Tekakwitha

The daughter of a fierce, pagan Mohawk warrior, Kateri was born near the town of Auriesville, New York, in 1656. She was four years old when her mother died of smallpox. Kateri also contracted the disease, and it disfigured her face. After her mother's death, two aunts and an uncle adopted her.

Through the efforts of Jesuit missionaries who brought the Catholic Faith to the Mohawk Valley, Kateri was converted as a teenager. Baptized at the age of twenty, she incurred the great hostility of her tribe. Although she had to suffer greatly for her Faith, she remained firm in it.

Kateri went to the new Christian colony of Native Americans in Canada. There she lived a life dedicated to prayer, penitential practices, and caring for the sick and aged. Every morning, even in bitterest winter, she stood before the chapel door until it opened at four and remained there until after the last Mass. She was devoted to the Eucharist and to Jesus Crucified.

She died on April 17, 1680, at the age of twenty-four. She was beatified in 1980 by Pope St. John Paul II and canonized by Pope Benedict XVI on October 21, 2012. The first Native American to be declared a Saint, she is known as the "Lily of the Mohawks."

July 14

St. Mary Magdalene

St. Mary, whom Jesus converted, and who witnessed His last moments with Mary, His Mother, and St. John, was called Magdalene from the town of Magdala in Galilee. She followed Jesus with other devout women during His public life.

In the darkest hour of her Lord's life, Mary stood at some distance, watching Him on the Cross. Then, with "the other Mary," she saw the great stone rolled before the door of the tomb in which the Lord's body was placed. It also was Mary who,

weeping by the sepulcher early on the first day of the week when she found His tomb empty, was the first to see the Risen Lord.

After His Resurrection, without which our Faith is vain, Jesus told Mary to go to the Apostles and tell them that He had risen. She went to the Eleven and told them of her encounter with the Lord.

July 22

St. Christopher

St. Christopher is one of the most popular Saints of the East and West. There are many often confused and contradictory legends concerning this Saint.

A composite story of the legends surrounding him tells of a very strong man named Offero who lived in the land of Canaan. His goal was to serve the mightiest of kings. Believing the devil to be the mightiest, he soon discovered that the devil feared Christ. Offero then decided to serve Christ.

While traveling, he met a hermit who guarded a dangerous passage across a stream and guided people to its safe crossing. The hermit taught him about Christ, the greatest King. Offero settled at this appealing spot, carrying travelers across the stream on his shoulders in order to well serve the great King.

As legends have it, one day he carried a small boy. Amazed at the weight of the little child, Offero told him that he felt as if he bore the entire world. The child told Offero that he was carrying Him Who created heaven and earth. According to legends, the Boy Jesus baptized Offero; from then on, he was to be called Christopher, that is, Christ-bearer.

Christopher is the patron of travelers. It is said that he died a martyr during the reign of Decius in the third century. *July 25*

St. Anne

St. Anne is venerated by the Church as the mother of the Blessed Virgin Mary and the grandmother of Jesus.

She and her husband, St. Joachim, lived in Nazareth and were devoted to God. Yet, when they had no children, the common belief was that God was punishing them.

When Anne seemingly was too old to have a child, their prayers for a child were at last answered. They called their daughter Miriam or "Mary." Anne offered Mary to the service of God at a very early age.

Anne has been honored from early Christian times. Churches were dedicated to her, and the Fathers, especially of the Eastern Churches, loved to speak of her sanctity and privileges. She is often represented as teaching her young daughter to read the Scriptures.

Her name means "grace." God gave Anne special graces; the greatest was that she was the mother of the Mother of God. It is no wonder that she is the patroness of mothers and of children.

Tradition relates that, in their old age, Joachim and Anne went to settle in Jerusalem; it was there that the Blessed Mother was born and reared. They also were buried there. A church was built during the fourth century, possibly by St. Helena, on the site of their home in Jerusalem.

July 26

St. Ignatius Loyola

St. Ignatius was born in Spain in 1491. Reared in the court of Ferdinand V of Aragon, he entered the army and served bravely. While recovering from wounds inflicted during the siege at Pamplona, he read lives of the Saints. Their stories prompted his conversion, and he chose to entrust his life entirely to God.

After confession at the monastery of Montserrat, Ignatius spent months of solitude in Manresa, where he composed his celebrated *Spiritual Exercises*. After a pilgrimage to Rome and the Holy Land, he began his studies in Spain. In 1528, he continued studying in Paris. There he joined with a few companions; they became the nucleus of the Society of Jesus, or the Jesuits, as they are more commonly known.

Ignatius and his companions were ordained in Venice, after which he went to Rome where he was graciously received by Pope Paul III, who approved the Society in 1540. Ignatius continued to reside in Rome, employed in consolidating and governing his Society, which he directed for some fifteen years. He died peacefully on July 31, 1556, and was canonized in 1622 by Pope Gregory XV.

The legacy of Ignatius lies not only in the *Exercises*, but in the work of the Jesuits: preaching, educating, conducting retreats, and ministering to God's people in need. *July 31*

St. Clare

Born in Assisi in 1193, St. Clare desired from her child-hood to devote herself to God. Inspired by the preaching of St. Francis, at eighteen she left home to go to the Portiun-cula, a small chapel where he prayed. There St. Francis gave her a simple habit and cut off her hair. He then sent her to a Benedictine convent.

Clare persevered despite family opposition. She triumphed; later her sister Agnes, her mother, and several other ladies joined her. They lived together in accord with a Rule that St. Francis gave them as a Second Order (or Poor Clares). In time, Clare became abbess of their monastery and founded several other monasteries, spreading her Order to Germany and Bohemia.

These religious women lived lives of prayer, work, poverty, simplicity, and almost complete silence—austerities rarely practiced among females at that time. In keeping with their spirit of poverty, Clare, as heiress to the large fortune of her father, gave all of it to the poor.

Defending her monastery against the attack of the army of Frederick II, she caused herself to be carried to a window, held the monstrance with the Blessed Sacrament in sight of the enemies, and prostrated herself before the Eucharistic God. The enemies, suddenly panic-stricken, fled in terror. She died on August 11, 1253, and was canonized in 1255 by Pope Alexander IV.

August 11

St. Maximilian Kolbe

Born in Poland in 1894, Maximilian became a Franciscan. He contracted tuberculosis in his early years; though he recovered, he remained frail all his life. Before his ordination, Maximilian founded the Immaculata Movement devoted to Our Lady. After receiving a doctorate in theology, he spread the Movement and helped form a community of eight hundred men.

Maximilian went to Japan, where he built a monastery; he then furthered the Movement in India before returning home in 1936. After the Nazi invasion in 1939, he was imprisoned and then released for a time. In 1941, he was arrested again and sent to the concentration camp at Auschwitz.

On July 31, 1941, in reprisal for one prisoner's escape, ten men were chosen to die. Father Kolbe offered himself in place of a husband and father and was the last to die, enduring two weeks of starvation, thirst, and neglect. He was canonized in 1981 by Pope St. John Paul II.

Present at the canonization was Francis Gajowniczek, the man whose life Father Kolbe saved. In an interview, he later recalled that when the camp commandant singled him out for execution, he cried out for his wife and children. At that point, prisoner 16670 asked to trade places with him. When Father Kolbe took his place, he went back to his spot. They exchanged no words—just a glance.

August 14

St. Stanislaus Kostka

St. Stanislaus was born of a noble Polish family in 1550. When he was fourteen, he and his brother, Paul, who was two years older than he, attended the college of the Jesuits in Vienna, Austria. Although Stanislaus was kind in spirit and a capable student, Paul nevertheless treated him badly while they were in school.

After two years at the college, Stanislaus became quite ill. He lived in the house of a Lutheran, and his landlord did not allow Stanislaus to call a priest to bring him the Eucharist in his house. He prayed to St. Barbara, his patroness, who appeared to him with two angels who brought him Communion. His healing came through the intercession of the Blessed Virgin Mary, who asked him to join the Jesuits. Because his father opposed the idea of Stanislaus becoming a priest, he had to leave Vienna.

He then traveled to Rome, where he lived for ten months as a model novice. Stanislaus welcomed the humble tasks he was assigned at the Jesuit College there and performed them cheerfully. It was during this time that he met St. Peter Canisius.

His devotion to Our Lady was profound. It was no doubt a great honor for him to die, at the age of seventeen, on the feast of her Assumption in 1568. *August 15*

St. Bernard

St. Bernard was born in Burgundy, France. He was sent at a young age to be educated at Châtillon, where he was recognized for his remarkable piety. There he began to study theology and Holy Scripture.

After his mother died, he entered the Cistercian Order. His brothers and several friends joined him. In 1113, with thirty young noblemen, Bernard presented himself to St. Stephen, the abbot of Cîteaux. He made his profession there the following year. Seeing his promise, his superior sent him with twelve monks to found a new monastery: the celebrated Abbey of Clairvaux. St. Bernard was at once appointed abbot and began the work that made him the most influential figure of the twelfth century.

His main objective was always to strengthen and spread the Faith. Thus, he founded numerous monasteries, penned many spiritual writings, preached eloquently, and traveled extensively. Both Popes and princes sought his advice.

Commissioned by Pope Eugene III to preach the Second Crusade, Bernard traveled through France and Germany, generating great enthusiasm for the Holy War among the masses. Though he endured great criticism when the Crusade was unsuccessful, people throughout Europe were inspired by this dynamic Saint. Bernard died on August 20, 1153, and was canonized in 1174 by Pope Alexander III.

August 20

74

St. Rose of Lima

St. Rose was born in Lima, Peru, in 1586, and given the name Isabel. She was confirmed with the name Rose by St. Turibius.

When her parents had financial troubles, Rose worked all day growing flowers and then sewed at night. To maintain her vow of virginity, she fought the wishes of her parents that she marry.

At twenty, she entered the Third Order of St. Dominic, living in virtual solitude in a small dwelling in the garden of her home. She modeled her life after that of St. Catherine of Siena, practicing extreme penance and mortification. She even wore a kind of crown of thorns on her head.

Jesus, Mary, and the Saints often appeared to her and confirmed for her that she had chosen a worthy life. Her extraordinary mystical gifts and visions prompted an examination by a commission of priests and doctors; they concluded that all of them were of supernatural origin.

Rose bore her many great adversities with heroic patience. In her later years, she used a room in her house to console the sick and suffering among the poor, Indians, and slaves. Her work was considered the beginning of social service in Peru.

She died in 1617 at thirty-one. In 1671 Pope Clement X canonized her, making her the first Saint in the Americas.

August 23

St. Augustine

St. Augustine was born on November 13, 354, at Tagaste in North Africa. Despite the piety of his mother, St. Monica, he fell into sinful ways and later became a heretic of the Manichaean sect. In 370, Augustine went to study at Carthage. His father, Patricius, who had been a pagan, died a year later, after converting to Christianity.

Subsequently, he taught rhetoric both at Carthage and in Milan. His conversion took place in Milan in response to God's grace, the prayers of his mother—who had followed him to Italy—and the influence of saintly friends, particularly St. Ambrose, who baptized him on Easter eve, in 387.

That same year, his mother died at Ostia. After returning to Tagaste, he began to live in community with some of his friends. Ordained in 390, he moved to Hippo. Five years later, he was consecrated Bishop and made coadjutor to Valerius, Bishop of Hippo, whom he succeeded the following year.

He worked tirelessly, governing his church, preaching to his people, and writing voluminous works that have been admired through the ages. His humility prompted him to write his *Confessions* about the year 397; from this work we have a detailed account of his early years.

This multifaceted religious genius and devout servant of God died on August 28, 430.

August 28

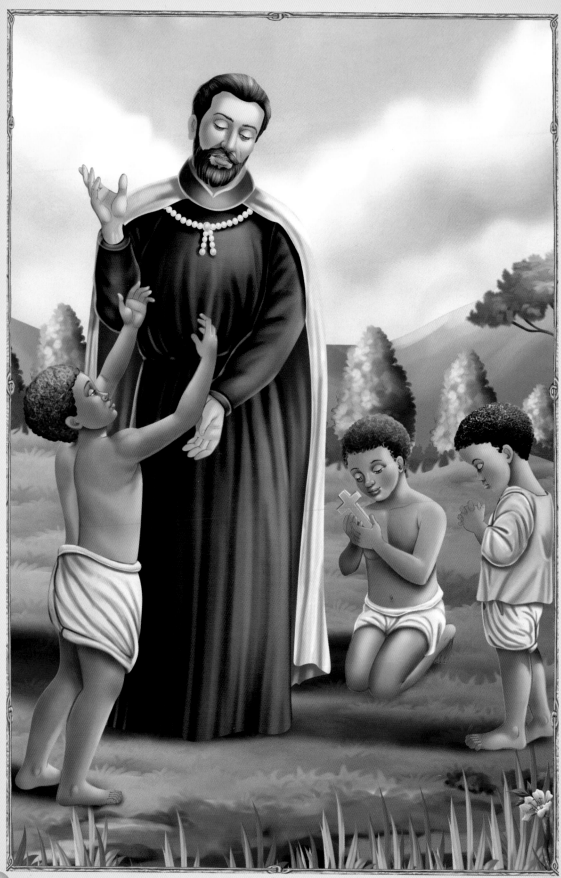

St. Peter Claver

St. Peter Claver was born at Verdu, Catalonia, Spain, in 1580. He studied at the Jesuit College of Barcelona, entered the Jesuit novitiate at Tarragona in 1602, and took his final vows on August 8, 1604. While studying philosophy at Majorca, he was influenced by St. Alphonsus Rodriguez to go to the Indies and save "millions of those perishing souls."

In 1610, he landed at Cartagena, the principal slave market of the New World. After his ordination in 1615, he dedicated himself to the service of the Black slaves, laboring tirelessly for their salvation and the abolition of the slave trade for a period of thirty-three years.

Boarding the slave ships as they entered the harbor, he hurried to quench the thirst of those held in unimaginable heat. He cared for the sick and dying and instructed the slaves through Black catechists; he then administered the Sacraments. Through his efforts, 300,000 souls entered the Church. Being fully committed to his converts, he followed them to the plantations to which they were sent, encouraged them to live as Christians, and prevailed on their masters to treat them humanely.

The Saint also preached in the city's main square, conducted missions with great success, and led an austere and holy life. Peter died in 1654 and was canonized in 1888 by Pope Leo XIII.

September 9

St. Vincent de Paul

St. Vincent was born of poor parents in the village of Pouy, France, about 1580. He was first schooled by the Franciscan Fathers at Acqs. Work as a tutor helped him continue his studies without burdening his parents. In 1596, he went to the University of Toulouse for theological studies, and there he was ordained a priest in 1600.

In 1605, during a sea voyage, he fell into the hands of African pirates and was carried as a slave to Tunis. Divine Providence enabled him to escape after nearly two years. He finally returned to France, where he tutored the children of the Count of Gondi.

Vincent began to preach missions in 1617, during which time he learned how badly the poor of France were being treated. He committed himself to improving their plight as well as that of prisoners and galley slaves.

In 1625, he founded the Congregation of the Mission (known also as Lazarists or Vincentians). Their work extended to preaching and education.

With St. Louise de Marillac, he established the Sisters of Charity to care for the sick, orphaned, and aged. He inspired works of charity that live on through the efforts of the St. Vincent de Paul Society.

Vincent died at age eighty on September 27, 1660. He was canonized in 1737 by Pope Clement XII. *September 27*

St. Jerome

Stridon, a small town on the border of Dalmatia, was the site of St. Jerome's birth about 347. As scholar, traveler throughout the Roman Empire, and acquaintance of leading Christians, he well prepared himself for great accomplishments.

He received Baptism at a then-customary mature age. At one point, he lived with the holy Abbot Theodosius in the desert of Chalcis in Syria, where he spent several years in prayer and study, including the study of Hebrew.

At Antioch he received Holy Orders about 377. After traveling in Palestine, he visited Constantinople, where St. Gregory Nazianzen was then Bishop. In time, he departed for Rome, where he served as secretary to Pope St. Damasus, who asked him to prepare the Latin translation of the Bible. This project took St. Jerome some twenty years and resulted in the Vulgate, which became the authentic text of the Bible for the Catholic Church.

Jerome's scriptural works, above all, are unparalleled. He also attacked the various errors of his day, especially with his pen. His fame spread far and wide, and he was a consultant to many in high places. After leading a full life, he died at Bethlehem in 420. Jerome is buried in St. Mary Major in Rome and was named a Doctor of the Church.

September 30

St. Thérèse
of the Child Jesus

Born at Alençon, France, in 1873, Thérèse Martin was the youngest of ten children and lost her mother when she was only four. Because of her great love for Jesus, she entered the Carmelite convent in Lisieux in 1888 at age fifteen.

Her life in the convent was very routine. At a young age, however, she learned the power of prayer, so spending her time in prayer and in performing the tasks required of her was her joy. Thérèse lived her life by her "Little Way": each day, she did ordinary things not only as perfectly as possible, but also with as much love as possible in order to please God. As a friend of Jesus, the Little Flower, as she came to be known, had a childlike love of God and trusted Him completely.

The story of her simple life in the convent is faithfully told in her spiritual autobiography, *The Story of a Soul*, which was published after her death. Every line is marked by the artless simplicity of a literary genius.

She courageously endured a painful condition of tuberculosis from which she died in 1897, at the age of twenty-four. In 1925, Pope Pius XI canonized Thérèse, and, on October 19, 1997, Pope St. John Paul II recognized her as the third woman Doctor of the Church.

October 1

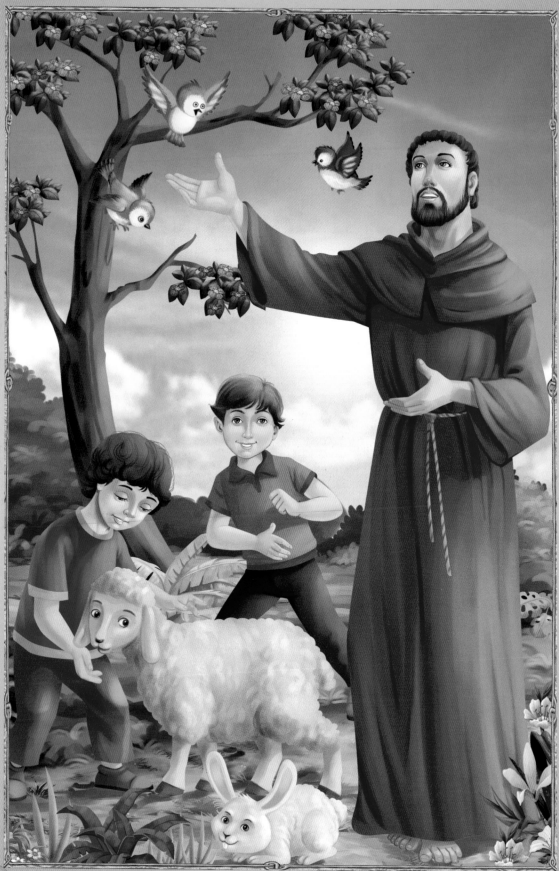

St. Francis of Assisi

Francis Bernardone was born at Assisi, Italy, in 1181. His father was a wealthy merchant there. During a time of imprisonment and then illness, Francis became aware of a vocation to a life of extraordinary service to the Church.

Inspired at twenty-five by Matthew's Gospel passage commanding the disciples to evangelize the world without possessions, Francis abandoned his affluent lifestyle and began to live a life of radical poverty. His example soon drew followers to his way of life.

In 1210, with twelve companions, he sought and received the approval of Pope Innocent III to lead a life according to the Rule of the Holy Gospel. Thus began the "Friars Minor," or "Lesser Brothers." Francis himself never became a priest out of humility, and at first only some of his band received Holy Orders.

Francis's practice of poverty and devotion to the humanity of Christ deeply touched a cold and weary world. Soon a vast Franciscan movement swept through Europe. By 1219, over five thousand Franciscans gathered at Assisi for the famed Chapter of Mats. Responding to this commitment to the Faith, Francis founded a Second Order for cloistered nuns through St. Clare and a Third Order for religious and laity of both sexes.

Francis died at sunset on October 3, 1226, and was canonized two years later.

October 4

St. Teresa of Avila

St. Teresa was born on March 28, 1515, in Avila, Spain. Her mother died when she was twelve, and her father placed her in a convent of Augustinian nuns. Shortly after she returned home—and against her father's objection—she entered the Carmelite monastery at Avila.

Her life was rich in prayer yet marked by struggle both within herself and in dealing with opposition from others. Graced by God, Teresa worked through her struggles to accomplish great things. She took on the task of reforming the Carmelite Order, restoring it to observance of the Rule on which it was established. In her zeal, and with the help of both St. John of the Cross and St. Peter of Alcantara, she succeeded in establishing over thirty new convents and monasteries throughout Spain.

While a woman of action, Teresa also was a contemplative who wrote letters and books that are classics of spiritual literature. Among them are her *Autobiography*, *The Way of Perfection*, and *The Interior Castle*. These and other of her writings have served to inspire and guide countless people on their spiritual journey.

Teresa's gifts were plentiful, and she used them all in total devotion to God. She was canonized in 1622 by Pope Gregory XV and made a Doctor of the Church in 1970 by Pope Paul VI.

October 15

St. Margaret Mary Alacoque

St. Margaret Mary Alacoque was born in the diocese of Autun, France, in 1647. Her family was well to do, but her father's death when she was young put her family in financial jeopardy at the hands of unscrupulous relatives. Though these were difficult times for young Margaret, her deep faith in, and devotion to, the Blessed Sacrament helped to sustain her.

Though she considered marriage, she ultimately joined the Order of the Visitation nuns in Paray-le-Monial at the age of twenty-four. Her life there was marked by further trial and tribulation, which she suffered with humility and dignity. Upon her profession, "Mary" was added to her name and she was henceforth called Margaret Mary.

From her youth, she had been favored with visions of Christ. These continued after she entered the convent. In later visions, Our Lord showed His Sacred Heart to her. The flames emitting from His Heart were a sign of His burning love for all people and His desire that they return that love. Jesus made twelve promises to St. Margaret Mary on behalf of those who would honor and love His Sacred Heart. Widespread devotion to the Sacred Heart was championed by her as well as by Claude de la Colombière, a Jesuit priest.

She died in 1690 and was canonized in 1920 by Pope Benedict XV.

October 16

St. Isaac Jogues

French Jesuits Sts. Isaac Jogues, John de Brébeuf, and their companions were among the missionaries who preached the Gospel to Huron and Iroquois Indians in North America. They were martyred by the Iroquois in the 1640s. Pope Pius XI beatified them in 1925 and canonized them five years later.

Isaac Jogues is outstanding among these martyrs. Ordained in Rouen in 1624, he became the first European to penetrate the eastern entrance of Lake Superior, one thousand miles inland.

After imprisonment, torture, and the loss of his hands there, he escaped the Iroquois with help from the Dutch. In 1646, he visited Auriesville, New York, to negotiate peace with the Iroquois.

On his third visit to the Iroquois, the Bear clan, believing he was a sorcerer, blamed him for an outbreak of sickness and the failure of their crops. As a result, this "Apostle of the Mohawks" was seized, tortured, and beheaded.

October 19

St. Martin de Porres

St. Martin de Porres was born at Lima, Peru, in 1579. His father was a Spanish gentleman and his mother an Indian woman from Panama. At fifteen, he became a lay brother at the Dominican Friary at Lima and spent his whole life there—as a barber, farm-laborer, distributor of alms, and caregiver, among other things.

He extended care to people of the whole city. Martin established an orphanage and a foundling hospital. In charge of distributing daily alms of food to the poor, he is said to have increased it miraculously at times. He also cared for the slaves brought to Peru from Africa.

He showed his all-embracing love equally to humans and animals—he even maintained a hospital for cats and dogs at his sister's house. Martin also possessed spiritual wisdom, demonstrated in his solving his sister's marital problems, raising a dowry for his niece inside of three days' time, and resolving theological problems for the learned of his Order and for Bishops.

Martin loved to fast and to pray—above all to pray at night in imitation of Jesus. During his whole life, whether he faced good times or bad, Martin always preserved a perfect serenity.

This saintly man died on November 3, 1639, and he was canonized in 1962 by Pope St. John XXIII. *November 3*

96

St. Charles Borromeo

St. Charles was born in Italy in 1538. He studied at Milan and afterward at the University of Pavia, where he received his doctorate in 1559. His uncle, the Cardinal de Medici, having been elected Pope that year under the title of Pius IV, made him Cardinal Deacon and administrator of Milan, though he was a twenty-two-year-old layman.

Because of his intellectual capabilities, Charles was given many key responsibilities within the Vatican before moving to Milan. Perhaps his most timely service to the Church was as Secretary of State, in which capacity he was instrumental in reassembling, in 1562, the Council of Trent (which had been adjourned for ten years), keeping it in session, and actively enforcing its reforms.

Ordained a priest in 1563, he was soon made Bishop of Milan, a city whose clergy and laity were in great need of reform. Knowing it was essential that he lead by example, Charles worked tirelessly to educate the clergy, establish the Confraternity of Christian Doctrine for the education of children, care for the poor, and preach eloquently to his flock.

In the great plague at Milan, he showed himself to be a true shepherd by personally ministering to the sick and dying. Charles died in 1584, at forty-six. He was canonized in 1610 by Pope Paul V.

November 4

St. Frances Xavier Cabrini

Frances Xavier Cabrini was born in Lombardy, Italy, in 1850, the youngest of thirteen children. At eighteen, she desired to become a sister, but poor health prevented her from doing so.

One day a priest asked her to teach in a girls' school; she stayed for six years. At the request of her Bishop, she founded the Missionary Sisters of the Sacred Heart to care for poor children in schools and hospitals. Then, at the urging of Pope Leo XIII, she went to the United States with six sisters in 1889 to work among the numerous Italian immigrants who had gone to America's shores.

Filled with deep trust in God and endowed with a wonderful administrative ability, she soon founded schools, hospitals, and orphanages and saw them flourish in service to countless Italian immigrants and children. Frances Xavier Cabrini founded sixty-seven institutions dedicated to caring for the poor, the abandoned, the uneducated, and the sick. She was called "Mother" because of her selfless care of so many. In order to accomplish her far-reaching work, she overcame a childhood fear of water and traveled across the seas more than thirty times.

She died of malaria on December 22, 1917. On July 7, 1946, she was the first American citizen to be made a Saint when canonized by Pope Pius XII.

November 13

St. Elizabeth of Hungary

St. Elizabeth was born to Alexander II, King of Hungary, in 1207. At the age of four, she was sent to be educated at the court of the ruler of Thuringia (a region of Germany), to whose infant son she was betrothed.

As she grew older, her piety increased in its intensity. In 1221, she married Louis of Thuringia and, despite her position, she began leading a simple life, practiced penance, and devoted herself to works of charity. Elizabeth's choice to abandon luxury and care for the poor was celebrated throughout Europe.

Her husband, a man of faith, encouraged her exemplary life. He was killed, however, while fighting with the Crusaders, leaving behind three children.

After his death, Elizabeth made arrangements for her children's care, and she then renounced the world and devoted herself to the care of the sick until her death in 1231. Pope Gregory IX canonized her in 1235.

November 17

St. Cecilia

According to her legendary *Acts*, St. Cecilia was a Roman native, born of patrician parents, and raised as a Christian. When young, she made a vow of virginity, but her parents forced her to marry a Roman nobleman named Valerian. By God's grace, although married, she preserved her virginity. Furthermore, she converted her husband to the Faith.

She also converted Tiburtius, her brother-in-law. During the Christian persecution, the two brothers secretly buried martyrs. They, too, suffered martyrdom for the Faith; Cecilia died in the same manner shortly after them. Their deaths occurred probably sometime between the years 161 and 192.

The circumstances surrounding the death of Cecilia have been drawn from legend. Ever dedicated to the Faith, she refused to sacrifice to the gods when challenged to do so by local authorities. She was to be put to death either by smothering or by being placed in a cauldron of boiling water, but the hand of God protected His servant. When this means did not work, a soldier was told to behead her. Although he struck her three times, she was badly wounded but remained alive for another three days. Only after receiving Holy Communion one last time did she succumb to death.

A famous and beloved Roman martyr, she is honored as the patroness of ecclesiastical music. *November 22*

St. Francis Xavier

Born in Navarre, Spain, in 1506, the "Apostle of the Indies" was of noble descent. At the age of eighteen, he went to Paris to study philosophy. About four years later, St. Ignatius Loyola came to Paris and lived at the College of St. Barbara, which Francis attended. Although Francis was full of worldly ambition, St. Ignatius influenced him greatly, leading Francis to become an early follower.

One of the first Jesuits, he was ordained a priest at Venice in 1537. Shortly after the Society of Jesus had been established, Francis was sent to Portugal. In 1541, he set sail for India, landing at Goa the following year. After his reform of Goa, his apostolic labors extended to the coast of Malabar, and to Travancor, Malacca, the Moluccas, and Ceylon; in all these places he converted large numbers to Christianity.

In 1549, he became the first missionary to Japan, where a flourishing Christian community soon arose. After remaining two years and four months, he then returned to India.

After visiting Goa, he set sail in 1552 to turn his attention to China. On the twenty-third day after his departure from Malacca he arrived at Sancian, an island off the Chinese coast. After a fever seized him, he died alone on a foreign shore on December 2, 1552, at forty-six. Francis was canonized in 1602 by Pope Clement VIII.

December 3

St. Stephen

St. Stephen, chosen after the Ascension as one of the seven deacons, was full of grace and fortitude and worked great signs. Many opposed him, but they were not able to withstand the wisdom with which he spoke so fearlessly.

Stephen was denounced to the Sanhedrin for blasphemy against God and against Moses because he had foretold the end of the Mosaic Law and the destruction of the Temple. Stephen's reply to these charges forms the longest speech in the Acts of the Apostles.

He summarizes the history of the Chosen People during the periods of the Patriarchs, Moses, David, and Solomon, solemnly professing his belief in God and his reverence for the Law and the Temple. He says that Abraham was justified and received God's favors; Solomon built the Temple, but God could not be confined in a handmade house; and the Temple and the Mosaic Law would stand only until God introduced more excellent institutions by sending the Messiah Himself.

So convincing was Stephen's speech that when he denounced the stubborn resistance put up by the people and exclaimed, "Look, I see the heavens opened, and the Son of Man standing at God's right hand," his hearers could take no more. They dragged him outside the city gates and stoned him in the year 35 A.D. *December 26*

St. Catherine Labouré

St. Catherine Labouré was born on May 2, 1806, in Burgundy, France. It is said that she was born as bells rang the evening Angelus; the day of her Baptism was the Feast of the Finding of the True Cross.

Later in her life, she visited a hospital of the Daughters of Charity and saw a picture of their founder, St. Vincent de Paul. Inspired by his commitment to the virtue of charity, Catherine entered the community of the Daughters of Charity in Paris, France.

After she had entered the convent, the Virgin Mary appeared to St. Catherine three times. In the first appearance, she was told that God was going to entrust her with a mission that would cause her great suffering, but that she would be given the grace to endure.

In the second and third appearances, Our Lady showed her the design of the medal of the Immaculate Conception, now known as the Miraculous Medal. She commissioned St. Catherine to have one made, and to spread devotion to this medal. With the help of her confessor, Father Jean Marie Aladel, she accomplished this mission. Only decades later did she reveal that Our Lady had given her the medal.

Catherine died on December 31, 1876, and was canonized on July 27, 1947, by Pope Pius XII.   *December 31*